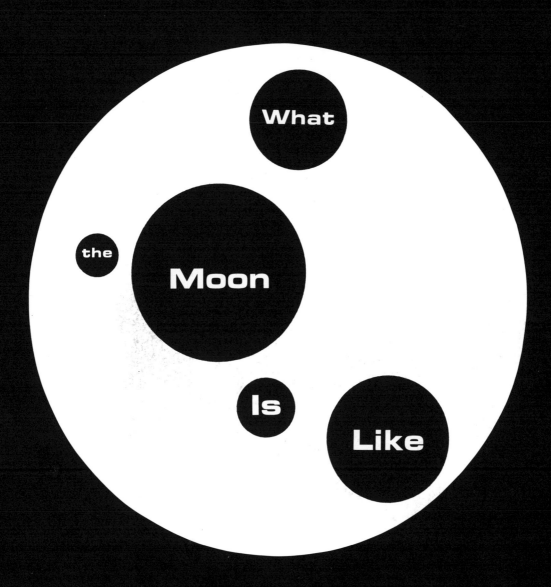

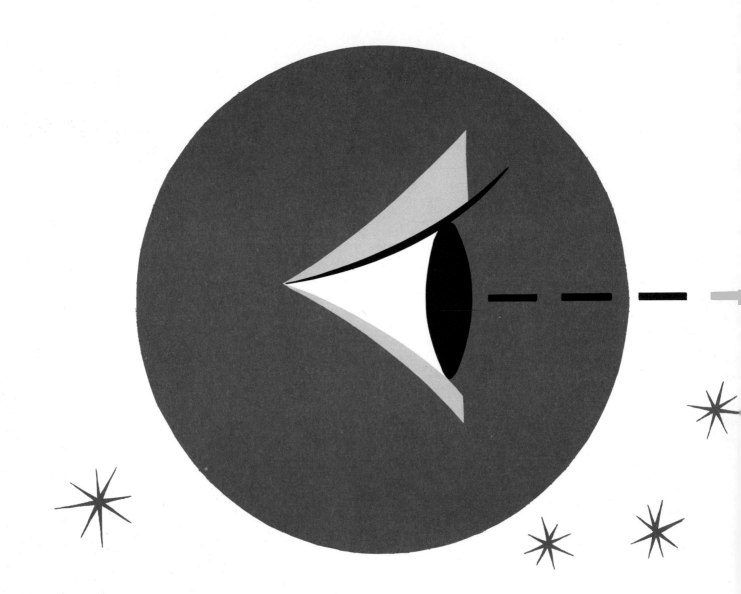

What the Moon Is Like

by Franklyn M. Branley

Illustrated by Bobri

THOMAS Y. CROWELL COMPANY   NEW YORK

LET'S-READ-AND-FIND-OUT SCIENCE BOOKS

Editors: *DR. ROMA GANS*, Professor Emeritus of Childhood Education, Teachers College, Columbia University

DR. FRANKLYN M. BRANLEY, Chairman and Astronomer of The American Museum–Hayden Planetarium

*AVAILABLE IN SPANISH

REC Library Edition reprinted with the permission of Thomas Y. Crowell Company

Responsive Environments Corp., Englewood Cliffs, N. J. 07632

WHAT THE MOON IS LIKE

Did you see the moon last night?
Was it big and round?

When the moon is round, people say they can see "the man in the moon."

The dark and light parts make them think of a mouth, a nose, and two eyes.

That is why they say there is a man in the moon.

Next time the moon is big and round, look at it.
The moon is far away, but we can see it very well.
We see that the moon is round like a ball.
Parts of the moon are bright. Other parts are dark.
Craters look bright. Seas look dark.
These are the bright and dark places you see when
   you look at the moon.

Make believe you are on the moon. What would it be like?

There is no air on the moon.

You cannot live without air, so you would need a space suit on the moon.

There would be air inside the space suit.

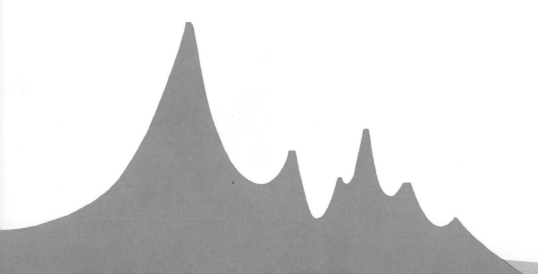

If you were in sunlight on the moon, it would be very hot. The space suit would keep you cool.

When you were out of the sunlight, it would be very
   cold.
The space suit would keep you warm.

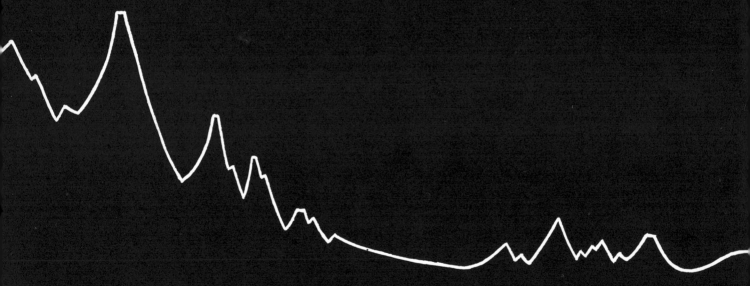

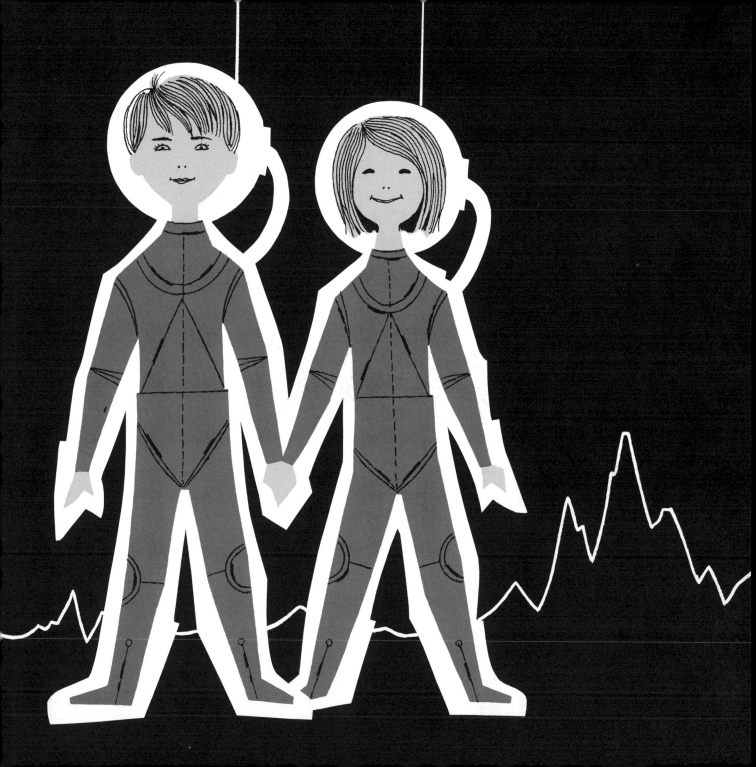

Do you weigh 60 pounds?

You would weigh only 10 pounds on the moon. So would your friend. You could pick him up easily.

You could pick up big rocks. You could throw them far, too.

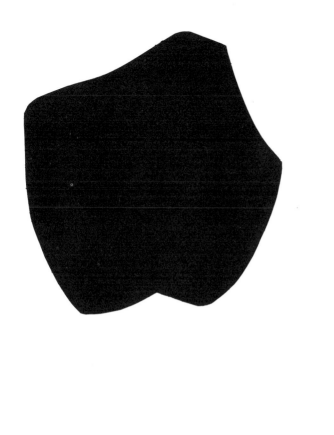

You could jump from place to place.
You could move easily in your space suit. You could
   jump right over a house, if there were houses on
   the moon.

You could explore the moon mountains. They are
   high and steep.
You could look into deep valleys. You would see
   rocks all over.
You could look into deep cracks in parts of the moon.
In the cracks you would see only rock and stone.

Nothing lives on the moon.

You would see no plants, flowers, birds; no grass, no animals.

You could explore the moon craters.
Craters are flat places with hills around them like a
wall.

Some craters are little. You could walk across them.
Other craters are big. One crater is one hundred
  eighty miles wide.
You could jump up the wall of a crater to see the
  other side. You would see more rock and stone.
  Maybe you would see a deep layer of dust, so deep
  that you would sink into it. Maybe you would see
  more craters.
Maybe you would see a lunar sea.

Lunar seas are big flat places on the moon.
We call them seas because they are flat, not because
they hold water. There is no water on the moon.

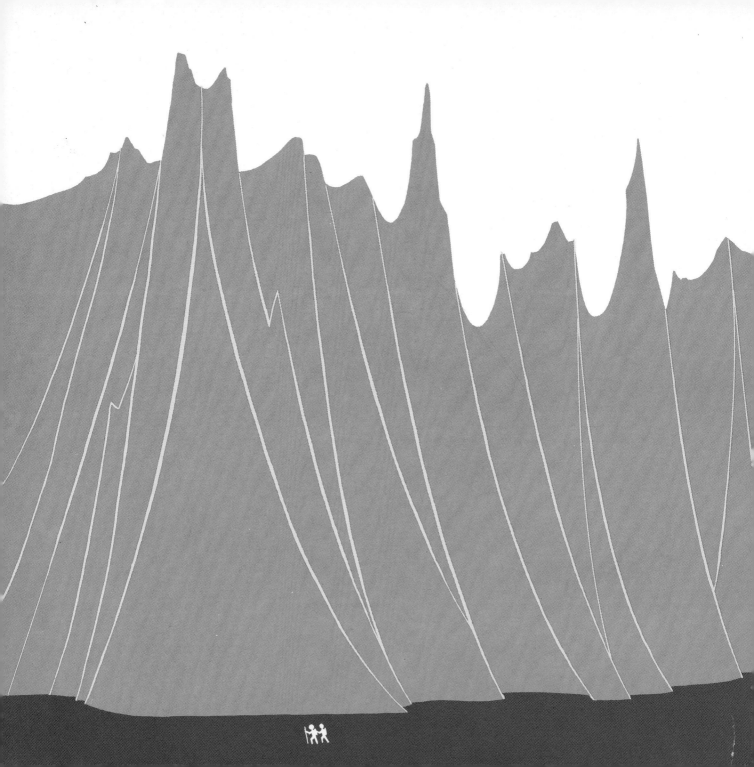

Some of the seas have high walls.
If you stood beside them, you would look very small.
Do you see the boy and girl in the picture?
That is how small you would look.

We want to know more about the moon.
We send rockets there to gather information and
send it to us.

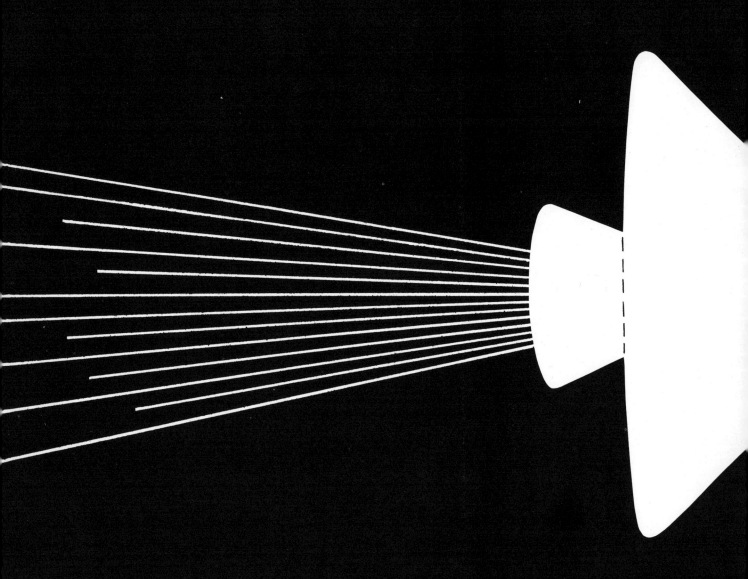

We send men to the moon.
They live inside the rocket that takes them to the moon.

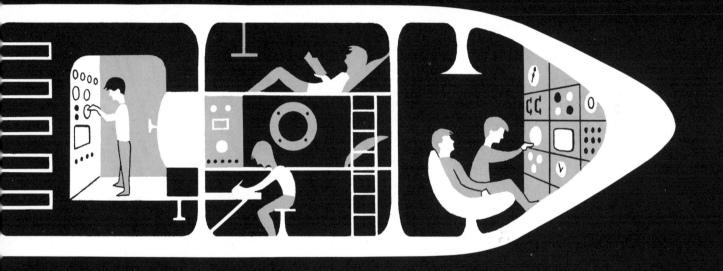

Outside the rocket the men wear space suits. The
   space suits keep them from getting too cold or too
   hot.
They take tanks of air with them so they can breathe.
They take water and food, too.

When men go to the moon, they explore the mountains, the deep cracks, the craters, and the seas.

They are moon explorers.

Moon exploring is exciting.
It is an adventure.
Some day you may be a moon explorer.

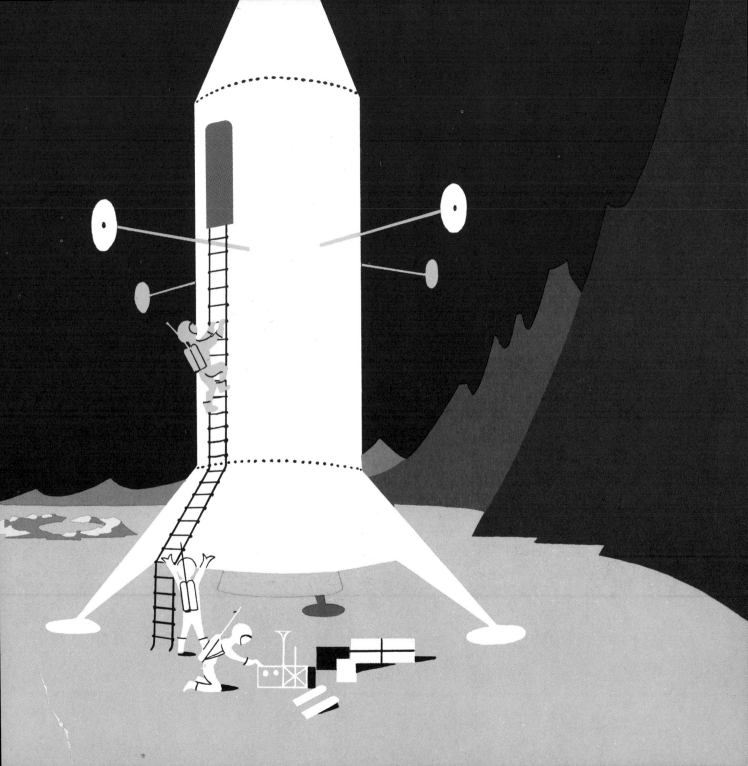

About the Author

Franklyn M. Branley is Astronomer and Chairman of the American Museum-Hayden Planetarium, where he has contact with audiences of all ages and where he directs the diverse educational program. For many years he has helped children learn scientific facts and principles at an early age and to develop their sense of wonder about the world they live in. Before coming to the Planetarium, Dr. Branley taught science at many grade levels; the lower elementary grades, high school, college, and graduate school.

Dr. Branley received his training for teaching at the State University of New York College at New Paltz, New York University, and Columbia University. He lives with his family in Woodcliff Lake, N. J.

About the Illustrator

Vladimir Bobri is equally at home—and well-known—in musical and artistic circles. He is president of the Society of the Classical Guitar, editor of *Guitar Review* magazine, and an acknowledged authority on gypsy music.

Mr. Bobri was born in the Ukraine where he attended the Kharkov Imperial Art School. He earned the money to come to this country in 1921 by making decorations and costumes for the Ballet Russe of Constantinople. Mr. Bobri has received a number of awards for children's book illustration as well as many citations from the Art Directors Club for his advertising design.